A QUICK GUIDE TO SCREENWRITING

A QUICK GUIDE TO SCREENWRITING

RAY MORTON

AN IMPRINT OF HAL LEONARD CORPORATION

Published in 2013 by Limelight Editions
An Imprint of Hal Leonard Corporation
7777 West Bluemound Road
Milwaukee, WI 53213

Trade Book Division Editorial Offices
33 Plymouth St., Montclair, NJ 07042

Printed in the United States of America

Book design by Mark Lerner

Library of Congress Cataloging-in-Publication Data is available upon
request.

ISBN 978-0-87910-804-5

www.limelighteditions.com

For Joe Romeo, my screenwriting buddy,
with friendship and appreciation

Contents

Introduction

Screenwriting is a very unusual craft—one that combines the ancient traditions of dramatic storytelling with modern cinematic technique into its own unique set of principles and protocols. This book lays out these conventions in simple, easy-to-read, and easy-to-understand fashion.

Unlike many other screenwriting tomes, this is not a dense compendium of inflexible rules or rigid formulas. Rather, it is a straightforward explanation of the key elements of cinematic narrative and formatting, along with a little history, a bit of essential business information, and some helpful advice and food for thought that, when mixed with your own imagination and creativity, will help get you started telling wonderful stories for the screen.

CHAPTER 1

What Is a Screenplay?

A screenplay is a written plan for a motion picture. It identifies all the settings and characters that will appear in the movie; describes the things those characters will say and do in those settings; and indicates the major props and effects (practical, visual, and sound) that will be required to realize those actions. The screenplay also lays out the order in which the events seen in the movie are to occur. In aggregate, all of these elements tell a dramatic story—a narrative in which a protagonist in pursuit of a significant goal becomes involved in a conflict that will eventually lead to climax, resolution, and ultimately transformation—that will (hopefully) engage, entertain, and move a reader and then, later—after it has been interpreted and realized by a team of skilled motion picture artists, technicians, and craftspeople—an audience.

In the world of professional screenwriting, there are three major types of screenplays:

1. *Specs*: Screenplays written on speculation (independently, without contracts or commissions) by screenwriters who hope to sell them to producers, production companies, or studios and/or use them as writing samples to secure representation or professional writing assignments.

2. *Assignments*: Screenplays that screenwriters are commissioned to write by a producer, production company, or studio. Assignments can involve creating original stories or crafting adaptations of existing works (novels, nonfiction books, comic books and graphic novels, board or video games, TV shows, earlier movies, etc.).

3. *Auteur scripts*: Screenplays written by directors who intend to realize these scripts themselves, usually independently (outside of the mainstream studio system). Auteur pieces are usually more personal or "artistic" in nature than regular specs and assignment scripts, and so tend not to go through the development process to the same degree the others do.

CHAPTER 2

A Brief History of Screenwriting

When movies first began in the late 1880s, the people who made them did not use screenplays. In fact, they didn't even use stories—movies then were just short documentaries that recorded real-life events (a man sneezing, workers leaving a factory, a train pulling into a station, etc.). The mere sight of pictures that moved was so astounding to early viewers that they didn't require anything else to be entertained. Eventually, however, the novelty wore thin and audiences began to want more.

By the early 1900s, filmmakers such as George Méliès in France and Edwin S. Porter in the United States had begun telling fictional stories in productions such as *Le Voyage dans la lune/A Trip to the Moon* (1902), *Life of an American Fireman* (1903), and *The Great Train Robbery* (1903). These early narrative films were just a few reels long and their stories were little more than sketches—brief melodramatic or comedic vignettes with simple setups, developments, and payoffs. There were no formal screenplays or screenwriters—the stories were usually conceived by the producer or the director and verbally described to the cast and crew on the set. If any narrative material was written down, it was usually just as a brief outline or précis.

When D. W. Griffith's *The Birth of a Nation* made its debut in 1915, the feature film (a movie running ninety minutes or more in length) was born. Along with it came the need for longer, more involved stories, and for a more formal way of presenting them. And so scenarios—detailed descriptions of all the scenes needed to tell a particular tale—began to be written for each production. Initially, directors, editors, and even continuity people did double duty as scribes, but as time went on, scenario writing became a specific profession all its own. Scenarists (as scenario writers were called) became integral members of a film's creative team.

Since movies were still silent, a way had to be found to convey information to the audience that could not be communicated visually. In the very early days of silent cinema, live narrators would stand next to the screen and tell the viewers what they needed to know. But before long, filmmakers began using inter-titles—cards with writing on them that were photographed and then inserted into the movie—to provide any necessary exposition and sometimes even brief snippets of dialogue. On occasion, these inter-titles were devised by the scenarist and written into the original scenario, but more often than not they were composed by a separate title writer, usually after the film had already been shot and edited (often changing the original intention of a scene and sometimes even the entire story).

The coming of sound in 1927 revolutionized screen-writing as much as it did the motion picture medium it-self. When pictures began to talk, the characters needed something to say, so the studios began recruiting Broadway playwrights—who were, by trade, masters of crafting strong and effective dialogue—to write for the screen. It was during this period that the terms *screenplay* and *screenwriter* came into common usage.

As a result of the playwrights' strong influence (as well as the limits imposed by early sound recording technology, which dictated that most scenes be staged around a single, immovable microphone), early talkies were often quite static and dialogue-heavy. However, as the playwrights became more experienced in working in their new medium (and as the technological restrictions lessened), the pictures they wrote became less talky and more fluid and visual.

When the studio system came into full flower during the 1930s and 1940s, most screenwriters (like most actors and directors) worked under contract for one company or another. Each studio had an official story department that acquired material with the potential to make exciting films—everything from original ideas by the screenwriters (and other industry professionals) to popular and classical plays and novels to short stories, magazine articles, and radio plays. When a studio decided to develop a particular property, the production chief would assign the project to a staff producer, who would then select a screenwriter from the studio's stable of contract scribes to convert the material into a script. In the early days of talking pictures, the ability to write a story and the ability to write dialogue were considered two separate skills and so, quite often, one scribe would craft a script's "continuity"—a scene-by-scene breakdown of the narrative in exacting detail—and another would pen the dialogue. By the 1940s, this division between dialogue and continuity writers had mostly disappeared and one screenwriter was usually responsible for all the elements in a script—for as long as they were on a project, anyway. (Then, as now, it was not unusual for a studio to employ multiple writers on a film to get the results they desired.)

When the studio system began to crumble in the late 1940s and early 1950s, many screenwriters lost their contracts and went freelance, working for studios and the increasing number of independent producers who began to populate the industry, on a picture-by-picture basis. (Some migrated to the new medium of television, although most TV writing in those early days of that medium was done by playwrights and former radio scribes.) The loss of job security was difficult for many screenwriters, but there were creative compensations. Coming out of World War II, audiences were hungry for more challenging material, and the film industry responded by making movies that tackled a much wider range of social, political, and personal issues than the medium had previously. This gave the screenwriters of these projects the opportunity to approach their work with greater maturity and depth than they had been able to before.

This trend continued into the 1960s. The elimination of the Motion Picture Production Code—the strict morality guidelines the industry had imposed on itself in the 1930s, in response to complaints from influential pressure groups who felt that violent and racy movies were setting a bad example for the nation—along with a more adventurous and permissive social climate, gave screenwriters license to explore a wide range of formerly taboo subjects with increasing frankness and, at times, wild experimentation. In the late 1960s, William Goldman's sale of his original screenplay *Butch Cassidy and the Sundance Kid* to Twentieth Century-Fox for a then-record $400,000 gave birth to a profitable spec script market that allowed screenwriters to create their own scripts independently and sell them to the highest bidder.

The 1970s proved to be a very important decade for screenwriters, who continued to explore increasingly challenging subject matter, with the stylistic experimentation of the 1960s giving way to a grittier, more realistic approach to action and dialogue. The spec market continued to grow, and the lessening power of the studios (which at this point were functioning primarily as financing and distribution entities, ceding most of the artistic direction of a film to its creative team) gave screenwriters unprecedented control over their work, while the rise of the "auteur" movement allowed many of them to direct their own material. Thanks to increased attention and appreciation from critics, film historians, and cinema studies professors, screenwriting—which had frequently been disparaged as glorified hackwork by "serious" writers—came to be regarded as a legitimate creative pursuit. Screenwriters, previously often dismissed as mere technicians under the heel of producers and directors, began to be taken more seriously as artists in their own right, with some, such as Goldman and Robert Towne (*Chinatown*), becoming as famous and celebrated as the stars and directors they worked with. All in all, it was a heady time to be a writer of moving pictures.

After a string of flop "auteur" films in the late 1970s and early 1980s, the studios reasserted their control over the moviemaking process, a move that had many negative ramifications for screenwriters. The bold experimentation of the 1960s and 1970s was over—as the cultural climate became increasingly conservative, the studios became primarily interested in conventional material executed in a conventional fashion, requiring screenwriters to rein in much of the creative ambition unleashed over the previous two decades. The spec market grew bigger and was more lucrative than ever, but only for material that was considered "high concept"—genre-based stories with broad, easy-to-grasp concepts that could be easily marketed. By this point in time, most of the studios had been taken over by conglomerates and had started to adopt the corporate cultures of their owners. As a result, most had added layers of bureaucracy to the development process—instead of dealing directly with the studio's production chief, screenwriters now had to run their material past a gauntlet of "creative executives" to get their work considered and approved. On the bright side, the increasingly blandness of mainstream material was countered by the rise of a vibrant independent film movement in the 1990s that gave screenwriters the chance to work on challenging material, albeit on a smaller scale and with lower budgets.

The first decade of the twenty-first century was also a difficult time for screenwriters. A huge increase in production and promotional costs prompted the studios to cut back significantly on the number of movies they made, which meant there were fewer scriptwriting assignments—and therefore less paid work—available. Because each film now required a huge financial outlay, the studios sought to minimize the risk to their investments by basing their productions on material that had already proven itself to be popular in other areas (and thus, it was assumed, had a guaranteed fan base that would turn out to buy tickets). This led to the production of more and more sequels to and remakes of previously successful films, and to more adaptations of best-selling books, old television shows, comic books and graphic novels, toys, board games, and video games. The studios had little appetite for original material, whose commercial appeal was unproven and thus considered too much of a risk. That, coupled with the collapse of the indie film movement, caused the once robust spec market to dry up.

Things are looking better in the 2010s. Although studios are still making fewer feature films than they once did, the spec market is starting to rebound and the digital filmmaking revolution—along with the growth of internet- and cable television–based distribution outlets such as Netflix, YouTube, iTunes, and the many video-on-demand channels—is beginning to resuscitate the independent film movement. In addition, the decade is also witnessing the birth of what may turn out to be an entirely new form of screen entertainment: movies made specifically for the many electronic devices—smartphones, tablet computers, MP3 players—that have become ubiquitous over the past ten years. Like short and feature films before them, these device-based pictures are going to require the skills and talents of experienced writers to adapt the classic tenets of dramatic storytelling to whatever the demands of the new medium will be, thus ensuring that the unique and wonderful craft of screenwriting will continue to thrive for years to come.

CHAPTER 3

Ideas

Every screenplay starts with an idea.

Where can you find ideas? Lots of places:

- Your imagination: Make something up.
- Your interests: What do you like? Do you like Ping-Pong? Then write a movie about Ping-Pong. Or mountain climbing. Or politics. Or brain surgery. Or anything else you feel passionate about. Drama can be found in just about every subject, and chances are, if you think something is interesting, other people will too.
- Your life: Take inspiration from your own experiences. Warning: It's not enough to simply write down something that happened to you—real-life events might be interesting, but that doesn't necessarily mean they are dramatic. To transform an actual happening into a great screenplay, you must find and emphasize the drama in that event. If there isn't any, you may need to introduce some fictional elements to provide it. Also, just because an occurrence has meaning for you, that doesn't mean

that it automatically will for your audience—you will need to find and highlight the universal truth in your experience to make the story as relevant to others as it is to you.

- The lives of others: The experiences of significant or interesting people can be fertile sources of material for a screen story. However, as with scripts based on your own adventures, you need to find the drama in your subject's biography. Many biopic authors write down every single incident that happened in their subject's life from birth to death and assume that's a story. It's not—as previously mentioned, real life isn't always (and in fact, almost never is) dramatic. To write a successful biopic you need to identify and highlight a strong narrative arc in your subject's chronology. As an example, consider 2012's *Lincoln*, which, rather than chronicling every event in the sixteenth president's life, chose to focus on a single dramatic episode in that life—Abraham Lincoln's struggle to pass the 13th Amendment. The movie told a story *about* Lincoln rather than the story *of* Lincoln, and its creative success was due in large part to that decision. If your subject's life does not contain a strong narrative arc, you will need to invent one. The 1984 film version of Peter Shaffer's play *Amadeus* contains a great deal of biographical information about the life of composer Wolfgang Amadeus Mozart, but it conveys that information through the largely fictionalized—and very dramatic—tale of how Mozart's jealous rival Antonio Salieri attempted to destroy him.

- Local, national, and world happenings, trends, and fads can all be excellent jumping-off points for a screenplay— *Erin Brockovich*, *All the President's Men*, *Kramer vs. Kramer*, and *Saturday Night Fever* are all good examples of scripts based on cultural topics that were hot at the time they were written.

- History: Events from the recent and distant past can also make exciting movies.

    Note: If you choose to write biopics or stories about current or historical events that feature actual living or recently deceased people, then you will need to give some thought to the matter of life rights, a.k.a. life story rights.

- In the United States, the First Amendment permits writers to write about any topic they choose, including other people. However, under U.S. law, citizens have a right to privacy (which includes the right to be left alone and the right not to reveal or have revealed previously undisclosed information, especially if it is of a compromising or embarrassing nature) and a right to control the commercial exploitation of their names and likenesses (the right of publicity), as well as protections against defamation (libel and slander). United States citizens are also entitled to sue if they feel that their rights in these areas have been violated. People cannot legally object to creative accounts that depict them accurately or that depict them participating in events that are part of the public record (occasions that have been chronicled in the media or in public domain documents such as court transcripts or recordings of public hearings), but they can object if they feel that the creative account portrays them inaccurately or violates their privacy. Just because a person objects to how a particular work portrays them does not necessarily mean he or she has a legitimate legal case, but even the threat of a lawsuit can be extremely costly.

To avoid legal entanglements, screenwriters can either sufficiently alter names and details, so that the characters seen on-screen cannot be mistaken for their real-life counterparts (this is often done in stories about actual occurrences in which the participants are not as important as the events themselves, but obviously defeats the purpose if the point of a script is to chronicle the life of a specific human being), or else they can acquire the real people's life story rights. Technically, no one actually owns the rights to his or her life story; what is really being acquired is the person's permission (in the form of a signed waiver drawn up by an experienced attorney) for him or her to be depicted in a script and on the screen. In exchange for some sort of consideration—usually a monetary fee—the subject signs a waiver that allows the filmmakers to use his or her name and character in whatever way they see fit (including fictionalizing story elements and character traits and revealing personal information) and promises not to sue over the results. Privacy and defamation rights expire upon a person's death, but in certain states and circumstances the right of publicity can be passed down, so arrangements may have to be made with the heirs of subjects who are recently deceased.

Obviously, these guidelines are for the United States only. Other countries have different laws regarding privacy, publicity, and defamation rights and remedies, and non-U.S. screenwriters should determine what laws govern these matters in their own lands before they start writing.

- Preexisting material: Filmmakers have been making adaptations of books, novels, short stories, newspaper and magazine articles, and other existing properties since the dawn of the cinema. It's easy to see why—the concepts have already been formed, which relieves the creative team of the burden of having to start from scratch, and the material has already proven it can connect with an audience (since people rarely adapt unsuccessful material), which makes it a much safer bet.

Before adapting a preexisting piece of material, you must first determine (with the help of an experienced attorney) if the property is in the public domain or under copyright. If the preexisting piece is under copyright, then you must obtain the screen rights to that material from the creator or current owner. If you are writing on assignment for a producer, production company, or studio, then it is their responsibility to do this before bringing you in on the project. If you are writing on spec, then you must obtain the rights yourself, before you write and especially before you attempt to sell your script, because it is illegal not to (since without those rights you would essentially be trafficking in stolen property) and because no legitimate buyer will even look at your work unless you can produce the necessary documentation to prove you are legally entitled to adapt the source material (any association with your script could make the buyer a target of whatever legal action that the owner of the purloined material may decide to take, and nobody wants that kind of trouble).

Optioning or buying adaptation rights can be expensive, but lawsuits are even more expensive (and can ruin your life and career). Don't make the mistake that some aspiring screenwriters do and submit a script based on unlicensed material in the hope that if a producer likes it, he will take on the burden and expense of obtaining the rights. He won't—it's too risky and too much trouble. It's much easier to simply not to bother. For sure don't do what some desperate writers have done and adapt an unlicensed piece of material and then change the surface details in an attempt to hide the theft—you will be found out, and that will certainly end your career and land you in a lot of hot water.

- Other movies: Whenever a movie is a hit, it's always followed by a string of imitations. That's understandable—people always want more of a good thing, and those who can provide it can potentially make a fortune. If you are approached by a producer to do a takeoff on a current hit, there's nothing wrong with accepting the job, as long as you put some sort of original spin on the material—it's okay to riff, but not to rip off. However, if you're considering penning a knockoff as a spec, you need to understand that, by the time any movie reaches the theaters, most of the industry has already seen it and has a sense of whether or not it's going to work. If the consensus is that the picture is going to be a hit, then there are probably already twenty imitations already in the works, and it will do you no good to be number twenty-one. When it comes to writing specs, it's probably best to try to anticipate the next trend, rather than to follow the current one. Whatever you do, don't write a spec sequel to a current hit. Many inexperienced writers do this because they hope the producers of the parent film will read their work and decide to use it as the basis for a follow-up. This will never happen. Most sequels are already under way before the original movie is released and, with rare exception, they are almost always developed in-house, usually using (at least to start) whoever wrote the final draft of the first installment to get things rolling on the follow-up.

For an idea to work as a screenplay, it must:

- Be able to be told in cinematic fashion: through action and images and dialogue (but not primarily though dialogue—talk-driven stories tend to be static, and movies need to move). Ideas that cannot be expressed in this manner should be developed in other formats (as plays, novels, short stories, etc.).

- Have commercial potential: Film is a very expensive medium—even a low-budget movie costs a lot of money to make. For a film's backers (whether a studio or private investors) to earn back their money and perhaps even turn a profit, the movie must attract a sufficient number of paying customers, so a viable screenplay idea is one with the potential to appeal to enough ticket buyers (and DVD and video-on-demand purchasers and cable TV subscribers) to generate revenue sufficient to at least cover the production's costs. Large-scale (and therefore big-budget) material—spectacular action and adventure films, special effects–dependent science-fiction and fantasy pictures, lavish period pieces, etc.—has to appeal to the widest audience possible; smaller-scale (and therefore smaller-budget) material—intimate dramas, topical stories, character pieces, "personal" films, etc.—can appeal to a narrower, more niche audience.

How can you tell if your idea is sufficiently commercial? You can never know for sure, of course, but in general commercial ideas tend to be those that are novel for their genre and market—that contain a new twist on an old concept or present a new concept in a traditional way (old concepts presented in traditional ways and new concepts presented in novel ways tend not to be commercial—viewers either find them to be tired or don't know what to make of them) and that can show audiences something they've never seen before. They also tend to be ideas that can generate juicy roles that will attract ticket-selling stars; that are set in some exotic milieu and so can take the viewers someplace new; and that provide ample opportunities for thrills, humor, spectacle, and/or tears—all of the elements that have traditionally engaged and excited audiences since the beginning of time.

- Be entertaining: The primary purpose of a movie is to entertain the people who watch it—to fully envelop audience members in an exciting experience that can hold their attention for 90 to 120 minutes; to present them with a sufficient number of the suspenseful and surprising twists, turns, and reversals that all good dramatic narratives offer; and to move them (emotionally, intellectually, or in a combination of the two) in some significant or memorable way, from making them feel that they have just taken the greatest roller coaster ride ever to prompting them to reconsider their entire philosophy of life. Movies can entertain in any number of ways—through spectacle, comedy, and thrills to be sure, but also by engaging viewers in more complex and challenging ways—by informing, provoking, intriguing, confounding, inspiring, disturbing, and transforming. Not every idea can do these things, but those that do have the potential to make excellent screenplays.

Initially, most screenplay ideas are very general: "I want to write a script about Ping-Pong." While this is a good place to start, a notion like this is too broad and lacks specificity. There are many different approaches you could take with such a vast conception: you could write an inspirational sports drama about a coach that transforms a ragtag group of kids into the greatest team of Ping-Pong players in the world. You could write a dark thriller about the owner of a Ping-Pong ball manufacturing company who plans to torch his own factory for the insurance money. You could write a romantic comedy about two competing Ping-Pong players who fall in love. Or you could write any one of hundreds of other variations on this one basic idea.

Obviously, you can't write all of those variations at once. So you have to narrow your general conception by selecting one specific "hook"—a single narrative conceit—from the hundreds of options your initial idea contains. This can be very difficult to do, because each variation will offer many wonderful possibilities for your story, and your first instinct will be to include them all. While this may be tempting, for practical reasons you can't—a tale that incorporated every possibility would be chaotic and incomprehensible. A successful story requires focus, and so you must choose. (Lawrence Kasdan, the great screenwriter of *Body Heat* and *Raiders of the Lost Ark*, once said that the most important thing that a writer does is choose.)

Once you have come up with a general idea and narrowed it down to a single hook, the next step is to craft a premise for that hook.

CHAPTER 4

The Premise

The premise is the fleshed-out version of your story concept.

A premise has two parts:

1. The Narrative Premise

The Narrative Premise is essentially a brief description of the tale you intend to tell. The Narrative Premise should lay out the following elements:

a. The Setup: the establishment of the story's hook—a shark attacks a beach resort; a giant ape is found on a remote prehistoric island and brought to New York City; a rich young man defies his powerful father to marry a poor young woman; etc.

b. The Protagonist: the main character of the story (sometimes called the Hero). The Protagonist has a significant goal that he or she wants or needs to achieve. That goal can be big (to save the world) or small (to save a local landmark); it can be internal (to overcome a trauma) or external (to find a buried treasure); it can be personal (to find love) or public (to stop global warming).

The Protagonist undergoes a profound transformation as a result of his or her experiences in the story (at its core, drama is always about transformation). This change is usually for the better—the Protagonist solves a personal problem, repairs a broken relationship, learns an important life lesson, achieves fame and fortune, etc.—although sometimes it can be for the worse—e.g., a good cop becomes corrupt; an idealistic woman becomes cynical; a sane man descends into madness. This transformation is often called the Protagonist's "arc."

In Hollywood, much is made of the need for the Protagonist to be "likable." This notion is based on the common wisdom that a movie will not be successful—either creatively or commercially—if viewers do not invest themselves emotionally in its story, and that they won't do that if they don't care about that story's protagonist. (This wisdom is essentially true—it's hard to spend two hours in the company of someone you have no feeling for.) Fearing that audiences will be turned off by a protagonist with negative qualities, many producers, studio heads, and movie stars often push for lead characters to be impossibly perfect, without flaws or blemishes of any kind. While it is easier for viewers to root for "positive" people, the success of films such as *The Godfather*, *Leaving Las Vegas*, and *Rachel Getting Married* show that they will also connect with "negative" characters, as long as those characters are charismatic and interesting and give the audience a reason to sympathize with them. Sympathy is the key—if we can find at least one reason to care about a character, then, no matter how flawed he or she is otherwise, we will be willing to invest ourselves in his or her plight. We care about Michael Corleone in *The Godfather* in spite of how awful he becomes because we can appreciate his sincere desire to save his father and protect his loved ones. We care about the Nicolas Cage and Anne Hathaway characters in *Leaving* and *Rachel* because we recognize that they are in pain and feel great empathy for their desire to find their way out of that pain, even if they can't quite figure out how to do so. So, if you want to write about a "negative" protagonist, go ahead—just be sure to give us a reason to care about him or her.

In a dramatic story, the actions the Protagonist takes in pursuit of his goal drive the story. Therefore, the Protagonist should always be active—he should do things rather than talk about doing things. He should not be passive—he should make things happen rather than react to events or the actions of others—because if the Protagonist is not active, then the story will be inert.

c. The Antagonist: a force that seeks to keep the Protagonist from achieving his or her goal. The Antagonist (sometimes called the Villain or the Bad Guy) is usually a person, but can also be a physical entity (a mountain that has to be climbed, a desert that needs to be crossed, a storm that must be survived), internal issues (phobias, a lack of confidence, an addiction), or circumstances (privation, imprisonment, oppression).

d. The Central Conflict: movies are a form of dramatic story-telling, and all dramatic storytelling is based on the conflict between the Protagonist, who is trying to get what he or she wants or needs, and the Antagonist, who is doing his/her/its best to prevent the Protagonist from getting what he or she wants or needs.

e. The Dramatic Question: to create tension and suspense, every dramatic story poses a narrative question that is generated by the characters and situations and that is answered by . . .

f. The Ending: which describes how the Central Conflict is ultimately resolved.

The following are the Narrative Premises of some classic films:

- *The Godfather*: After an attempt is made on the life of powerful Mafia boss Vito Corleone by rival gangsters seeking to take over his criminal empire, Vito's idealistic son Michael, who has spent his life trying to distance himself from his father's life of crime, ends up taking Vito's place as the head of the Corleone crime organization. Will the young man be able to defeat Vito's enemies and save his family without losing his soul? After seemingly being defeated, Michael launches a surprise attack against the rival gangsters and eliminates them, but in the process becomes more corrupt, ruthless, and evil than his father ever was.

- *Star Wars*: A long time ago, in a galaxy far, far away, Luke Skywalker, a farm boy from the remote planet of Tatooine, joins a mystical warrior named Obi-Wan Kenobi on a mission to rescue the beautiful Princess Leia. The princess—the leader of a rebel insurgency—has been taken prisoner by agents of the evil Empire that rules the galaxy. During the mission, Luke is told that if he can learn to trust his feelings, he will be able to develop the same mystical powers as Obi-Wan. Will Luke learn to sufficiently trust his feelings? At first he finds it difficult to let go of practical concerns, but during a final dogfight in outer space, Luke is finally able to put his faith in his emotions and uses the powers he develops as a result to successfully combat and ultimately defeat the Empire.

- *Casablanca*: Expatriate American Rick Blaine was once an idealist who fought for a number of noble causes, including freedom in Spain and Ethiopia, and with the resistance in Paris. However, after his lover Ilsa jilted him, he became bitter and disillusioned and vowed to never again stick his neck out for anyone. After escaping from France, he eventually becomes a nightclub owner in the Vichy-controlled Moroccan city of Casablanca. One night in the early days of World War II, Ilsa enters Rick's nightclub with her husband, Victor Laszlo, the leader of the Czech resistance. Ilsa asks Rick to help Laszlo and her escape from the Nazis. Will Rick overcome his personal disappointment and bitterness in order to help Laszlo and, by extension, the cause of freedom? After initially refusing to help, Rick eventually reverses course. He deftly engineers the couple's escape, recovers his idealism, and departs Casablanca to resume fighting the good fight.

You will need to conceive similar capsules for your own ideas. Possible narrative premises for our hypothetical Ping-Pong stories could be:

- After being convicted for drunken driving, Bill Thompson, a bitter ex-Ping-Pong champ whose career was ruined by excessive boozing, is given the chance to avoid jail if he agrees to coach a motley group of misfit kids at an inner-city rec center. Initially Bill goes about his task halfheartedly, doing only enough to stay out of prison.

But when he realizes that the kids look up to him and believe in his ability to coach them to a world championship, he is inspired to clean up his act and really get to work. He transforms his charges into a crack team that wins the chance to travel to Beijing to compete against players from all over the world in a high-stakes international Ping-Pong tournament. Will Bill maintain his newfound sobriety and positive outlook? After a humiliating encounter with an ex-rival, Bill falls off the wagon and fails to show for a key match, causing his team to forfeit. Knowing he let the kids down, Bill prepares to quit—but when his charges make it clear that they still believe in him, Bill pulls himself together once and for all and leads the team to victory.

- In desperate need of a large amount of money to maintain his opulent lifestyle, Dick Davis, the owner of a Ping-Pong ball manufacturing company and a pillar of his community, hires a local mobster to burn down his factory so that Davis can collect the insurance money. All goes as planned, but then the mobster begins blackmailing Davis into using his civic, business, and society connections to help commit a series of increasingly serious crimes. Can Davis maintain his upstanding façade even as he is being drawn deeper and deeper into the criminal underworld? Initially he is able to, but when the mobster refuses to let Davis out of their arrangement and the Ping-Pong ball manufacturer turns to murder to resolve the situation, his crimes are uncovered and his once perfect life crumbles.

- Ace Martin—the top men's Ping-Pong player in the U.S.—and Katie McIntosh—America's top female player—meet during an exhibition match. After each shows up the other, they take an instant dislike to one another. However, they meet again while playing on the national circuit and this time they fall in love, much to the consternation of their friends, family, and coaches, who feel that their romance will distract them from their careers. In spite of all of the opposition, Ace and Katie's romance continues to grow, until a competition rule change finds them facing off against one another in a championship match for the world title. Each wants the other to drop out, but both refuse. They get into a big fight over this, which ends with them breaking up. Will their individual desire to be the world champ destroy their love? As the match begins, it looks as if it might. But as the competition progresses, they realize how strong their love is, and both decide to throw the match at the same time. In the end, they lose the title, but gain each other.

2. The Thematic Premise

The Thematic Premise is the point of your story—the underlying theme or "message" or "moral" that the narrative is meant to convey. The Thematic Premise gives the story its purpose—it is the reason the tale is being told.

Every story has a Thematic Premise—some are overt and some subtle; some are simplistic and some complex. The Thematic Premises for the classic films mentioned above are:

- *The Godfather*: You cannot resist destiny.
- *Star Wars*: If you trust in yourself, then there's nothing you can't accomplish.
- *Casablanca*: If you abandon your ideals, you will be defeated. If you hold on to them, you will triumph.

Here are some possible themes for the Ping-Pong premises mentioned above:

- Redemption is possible when we learn to believe in ourselves as much as others believe in us.
- No matter how good a life you lead, once you start down a dark path, there is no turning back.
- Love is stronger than ambition.

Some screenwriters come up with the Thematic Premise for their story first and then construct their Narrative Premise around it. Some come up with the Narrative Premise first and discover the Thematic Premise as they write. There is no one right way to go about it, as long as you end up with both—because without a Thematic Premise, you will have a story without a point; and without a Narrative Premise, you will have a point without a story.

CHAPTER 5

Constructing the Plot

Once the premise has been developed, it's time to construct the plot—the structured series of events that expands the premise into a complete story.

Most movie plots follow a very specific template—one based on the core principles of dramatic writing first set down by Aristotle in ancient Greece and refined by playwrights and screenwriters over the course of the ensuing millennia. This template contains all the key elements of dramatic storytelling—exposition, rising action, climax, falling action, and denouement—as adapted for the specific demands of the cinema. It has been at the core of just about every creatively successful screenplay ever written, from *Citizen Kane*, *Gone with the Wind*, and *Bringing Up Baby* to *Rocky*, *Raiders of the Lost Ark*, and *The Terminator* to *Schindler's List*, *The 40-Year-Old Virgin*, and *The Social Network*.

According to this template, a screen story is divided into three sections called *acts*. (Some screenwriters prefer to divide their stories into more than three sections; however, no matter what the apportionment, the ingredients and overall structure remain the same.) The three acts of a screen story unfold as follows:

ACT I
- The world the story takes place in is established.
- The Protagonist is introduced and his circumstances are laid out.
- Key supporting characters, the relationships between the characters, and additional important story elements are also established.
- A crucial event occurs that sets the story in motion. This event is called the inciting incident. In *The Godfather*, the inciting incident occurs when Vito declines Sollozzo's request to back his drug business; in *Star Wars*, it occurs when R2-D2 and C-3PO escape with the stolen Death Star plans and land on Luke Skywalker's home planet; *Casablanca*'s inciting incident occurs when Ilsa walks into Rick's cafe for the first time.
- At the end of Act I, something happens that changes the Protagonist's situation in some very drastic way. This event is called the catalyst. It is also known as the first plot point, the first turning point, the first plot twist, the Act I plot twist, or the complication. The shooting of Vito Corleone is the catalyst in *The Godfather*; in *Star Wars*, it is the murder of Luke's aunt and uncle; in *Casablanca*, it is when Victor Laszlo asks Rick to sell him the letters of transit.

- As a result of this catalyst, the Protagonist develops a significant goal he becomes determined to achieve. In *The Godfather*, Michael's goal is to protect his father and family; in *Star Wars*, Luke's goal is to learn the ways of the Force and become a Jedi Knight; in *Casablanca*, Rick's goal is to remain neutral and uninvolved.

ACT II

- The Protagonist—usually working against some sort of tension-generating, "ticking clock" deadline—develops a plan for accomplishing his goal and then sets out to follow it.
- The Protagonist's quest to achieve his objective brings him into contact with the Antagonist, who is or becomes determined to stop the Protagonist from accomplishing his goal.
- During his quest, the Protagonist encounters a series of obstacles—primarily generated by the Antagonist—that stand between him and his objective.
- The Protagonist usually begins Act II at a disadvantage (caused by the catalyst), but uses his inner and outer resources—which can include special skills and abilities and help from unusual allies—to overcome these obstacles (which become bigger, more complex, and more difficult to deal with as the narrative progresses) and begin to march toward victory.

- Near the end of Act II, the Protagonist closes in on that victory. He reaches a point where it appears that he is about to achieve his goal. Success seems to be within his grasp.

- At this point, something happens that once again drastically changes the Protagonist's circumstances. This event robs the Protagonist of his impending triumph and leaves him in a defeated (and often precarious) position, facing a new obstacle so formidable that it appears that he will never be able to overcome it and, as result, will fail to ever accomplish his goal. This event is known as the *catastrophe*. It is also known at the second plot point, the second turning point, the second plot twist, the Act II plot twist, the second complication, or the crash-and-burn. In *The Godfather*, the catastrophe comes when Vito is forced to give in to Barzini's demands following Sonny's assassination; in *Star Wars*, the catastrophe is the death of Obi-Wan Kenobi, followed by the realization that the Empire has tracked the rebels to their secret base; in *Casablanca*, it is when Laszlo is arrested.

ACT III

- As Act III begins, all hope appears to be lost. The Protagonist has been defeated, and it seems as though he will never be able to achieve his objective.

- At this point—when the Protagonist is at his absolute lowest—something happens that allows him or motivates him to rally.
- The Protagonist now does one of two things: he either comes up with a new plan to achieve his original objective, or else he abandons that objective and comes up with an entirely new goal (and a plan to achieve it). For example, in *Casablanca*, Rick forgoes his desire to remain neutral and instead becomes determined to help Ilsa and Laszlo escape.
- The Protagonist sets out to put his new plan into action.
- This leads to the story's climax—a final confrontation with the Antagonist in which the Protagonist is finally able to overcome the seemingly insurmountable obstacle—usually by defeating the Antagonist—and accomplishes his goal (if the story is a comedy) or fails to accomplish it (if the story is a tragedy). The climax of *The Godfather* comes when Michael wipes out all of the family's enemies in a surprise mass attack; the climax of *Star Wars* is when Luke turns off his targeting computer and uses the Force to torpedo the Death Star; in *Casablanca*, the climax begins when Rick pulls a gun on Renault, and comes to a head when he sends Ilsa off with Laszlo.
- Act III concludes with the resolution, which shows how all of the story's problems are resolved and how things

work out for all the characters as a result of the climax. The resolution often indicates how things are expected to go for the characters after the story ends. *The Godfather* resolves with Michael assuming control of the Corleone family and empire; *Star Wars* concludes with Luke becoming a hero; and *Casablanca* finishes with Rick and Renault setting out to fight Nazis.

You should use this template to guide you when you are constructing your plot. There are some who may object to this recommendation, dismissing the template as a rigid formula and insisting that following it will constrict their creativity and result in a routine, by-the-numbers product. This is not the case.

- This template is not a formula. Rather, it is a base—a very solid base that contains all the elements required to create a strong dramatic narrative. (Writing that does not contain these elements may be very good, but it will not be drama—these elements used in this configuration is what makes a piece of writing a drama, as opposed to prose or poetry.) Using it will ensure that whatever tale you tell will be dramatically sound.
- It is very adaptable. This template can be and has been used successfully to construct every conceivable type of screen story. It can be used to create historical dramas,

contemporary issue films, romantic comedies, farcical comedies and spoofs, thrillers, mysteries, musicals, action movies, horror films, science-fiction epics, biopics, and so on. Following this template will not restrict the types of stories you can tell—rather, it will allow you to tell any tale you like.

- It's not rigid. Quite the opposite—this template is enormously flexible. It can be followed exactly in a very straightforward manner; it can be broken up, twisted around, and turned inside out (such as in the nonlinear, narrative-bending screenplays of Quentin Tarantino or Charlie Kaufman); pieces of it can even be left out. (William Goldman's script for *All the President's Men* famously stops at the end of Act II. History—our common knowledge as to how the Watergate affair turned out—provides the third act.) It can be duplicated for scripts with multiple story lines (such as *American Graffiti* and *Love Actually*) and encapsulated for episodic scripts (such as *Boogie Nights*). It can be stretched to accommodate numerous twists and surprises and even the occasional digression. Using this template will not restrict the way in which you tell your story—it gives you the freedom to tell your tale in any way you like.

If you think of this template as a tool to aid your creativity rather than a barrier to restrict it, then you will find it to be an enormous help as you attempt to construct an original and effective screen story.

The following elements should be incorporated into the plot as it is being constructed:

1. The Protagonist's Arc

The Protagonist's starting position—the place from which he will begin his transformation—should be established in Act I. This is done by dramatizing that position—usually by giving the Protagonist a problem or dilemma caused by the starting position. For example, the protagonist of *Die Hard*—New York City police detective John McClane—is an unsupportive husband who eventually transforms into a supportive husband. His starting position is dramatized by establishing that his wife, Holly, left him because he refused to move to Los Angeles with her after she received an important promotion.

This problem should continue to be an obstacle for the Protagonist throughout the story. At the beginning of *Die Hard*, McClane comes to Los Angeles to meet with Holly and hopefully persuade her to reconcile. She is initially open to the idea, but McClane continues to be unsupportive and alienates her all over again.

At some point during Act II, the events of the story force the Protagonist to recognize that he needs to change. In *Die Hard*, McClane—faced with the possibility that he might lose

Holly to the terrorists who have taken over the office build-ing in which she works—admits to his ally, LAPD Sergeant Al Powell, that he has been a bad and unsupportive husband and expresses his regret he didn't do things differently in the past, which indicates that he now knows he needs to start doing things differently.

At a key point in the story (sometimes at the climax, sometimes prior to the climax in order to set the stage for it), the Protagonist changes. This is called the *moment of transformation*. McClane's moment of transformation comes when—realizing he might not survive his war with the terrorists—asks Powell to apologize to Holly on his behalf if he doesn't make it. With this action, McClane renounces his old, unsupportive ways and announces his intention to pursue a different path in the future (should he have one).

The Protagonist's change then needs to be demonstrated. McClane does this near the end of the story by introducing Holly to Al using her professional name—Holly Gennaro—a clear sign that he now supports her in her career objectives.

The impact that the Protagonist's transformation will have on his life beyond the events of the story must also be demonstrated. This is usually done in the story's resolution. In the resolution of *Die Hard*, the impact that McClane's transformation will have on his future is demonstrated when Holly introduces herself to Powell using her married name—which tells us that, because McClane has changed, Holly will reconcile with him and they will now have a happier marriage.

The Protagonist's transformation should always come about as a result of the events in the story. In *Die Hard*, McClane would not have changed his ways if the terrorists had not taken over the building and he was not faced with the prospect of losing his wife. The events of the story had to happen for McClane's change to occur. Compare this with the transformation of Martin Riggs in *Lethal Weapon*: Riggs begins the film on the verge of killing himself and ends it no longer feeling suicidal—a welcome change, to be sure, but one that is imposed on the story rather than brought about by any of its events. While Riggs' suicidal disposition is established in Act I of *Lethal Weapon* and continues to be a problem in Act II, there is no point in the story where his need to change is acknowledged, nor is there any moment of transformation (although there are several resolutions). McClane's change is earned, while Riggs' is essentially tacked on (a rare flaw in an otherwise strong screenplay), which makes it less satisfying.

Other characters in the script can also undergo transformations (for example, a criminal Antagonist can learn the error of his ways and decide to go straight at the end of a caper movie), but their arcs should never be bigger or more significant than that of the Protagonist.

2. Genre Obligations

Many film stories are genre stories. Major movie genres include: Action; Adventure; Thriller (Detective, Crime, Caper, Psychological); Comedy (Romantic, Screwball, Buddy, Underdog, Spoof); Drama (Social Issue, Courtroom, Medical, Family); Mystery; Horror (Monster, Supernatural, Slasher); Science Fiction; Fantasy; Western; Sports (Comedy or Drama); and Biopic. Every genre has certain specific narrative and structural elements and conventions that must be included in a plot for it to be considered part of that genre. For example:

- Romantic Comedies must have a "cute meet"—a scene in which the two leads first encounter each other in some quirky or amusing fashion. There must also be an unsuitable suitor for one of the leads to throw over when he or she finally gets together with the other lead, as well as a silly misunderstanding that causes the two leads to break up at the end of Act II, so they can get back together at the end of Act III.

- Sports Movies always feature an underdog player or team no one thinks can win; an unconventional coach who is the only one who believes in the player or the team; a rival player or team that appears to outmatch the underdog in every way; a training sequence in which the underdog player or team gets up to speed; and, of course, a final game or match in which the underdog takes a terrible beating before coming from behind against all odds to win.

- Fantasy films usually present a callow young hero who receives a call to adventure that he first rejects, and then later accepts; a mentor who informs the hero that he possesses some sort of amazing power and then teaches him to use it; a villain with powers that rival the hero's; a beautiful young woman for the hero to rescue and romance; and a final battle in which the forces of good clash with and eventually triumph over the forces of evil.

- Mysteries always have a murder, a red herring, and a "revealing the culprit" scene; Courtroom Dramas always climax with a big trial; Thrillers and Action movies usually feature car chases, fistfights, and a valuable MacGuffin (the object everyone is searching for or fighting over); and so on.

When crafting a genre story, you must address these elements and conventions in some fashion in your plot. You can employ them as expected (which will certainly ensure that your story fulfills genre expectations, but could result in a piece that feels stale or clichéd); you can twist the required items in clever, unexpected ways (this can make the piece feel fresh, as long as you don't twist them so far that the genre is no longer recognizable); you can spoof them; or you can subvert them. The only thing you cannot do is ignore them, because audiences—whether they are conscious of it or not—know all of these obligatory elements and are expecting them (part of the fun of watching a genre film is to see how the conventions will play out). If you leave them out (which some writers do, thinking they are solving the cliché problem by avoiding it), the viewers will be disappointed and leave the movie feeling unsatisfied.

3. Subplots

Story elements that are relevant to the overall tale but don't fit smoothly into the primary narrative are often addressed in subplots. Subplots are exactly what their name implies: short plotlines contained within the main story. They are constructed in the same manner as the main plot: they have three acts that include catalyst; conflict; a catastrophe; a climax; and a resolution. Subplots are used to:

- Provide exposition that cannot be easily introduced through the events in the main plotline
- Develop the Protagonist by showing another side of him (e.g., by chronicling a relationship with an Example character, or by having him fight for a noble or ignoble cause, or by showing him struggle with a personal issue); by providing him with a reason to participate in the main story (e.g., the Protagonist decides to pull off a big heist in order to pay the enormous medical bills generated by

the ongoing treatment of his child's mysterious illness); or by showing the impact of the main story's events on the Protagonist's personal life (e.g., their effect on his marriage or other relationships; the temptation they present for him to start or resume drinking; and so on).

- Develop a supporting character.
- Provide a counterpoint to the themes or action of the main story.

A subplot should only be included in a screen story if it serves one of these purposes; they should never be extraneous or superfluous. Subplots should not be as complex or developed as the primary narrative, nor should they ever overshadow it.

CHAPTER 6

Additional Storytelling Elements

SCENES

To tell a screen story, the overall plot is broken down into individual units called scenes. A scene is a dramatization of one or more of the events that make up the story. The purpose of a scene is to advance the plot, either by adding a new link to the narrative chain or by introducing an important piece of exposition (information needed to understand the story). Any scene that does not movie the plot forward should not be in the screenplay.

A narrative scene should be structured like a miniature plot—there should be a protagonist and antagonist, a catalyst, central conflict, catastrophe, climax, and resolution. It should also be well paced, beginning as close to the catalyst as possible and ending as soon after the catastrophe as possible.

Exposition can and should be incorporated into narrative scenes, delivered as part of the dramatic action, whenever possible. However, exposition is sometimes introduced in stand-alone scenes that are purely illustrative—that exist simply to show us something (a clue, geography, how something works) in a clear and memorable way, so we can recall it later when the plot demands. Because expository scenes lack the drama of narrative scenes, they should be as brief as possible, so as not to slow the pace of the overall story.

The number varies depending on the tale being told, but the average feature-length screenplay usually contains somewhere between fifty and sixty scenes.

STORYTELLING DEVICES

Screenwriters can employ a number of different devices to help tell their stories:

- Suspense: This device creates tension through anticipation—by telling viewers that something significant, often something terrible or terrifying, is about to happen, and then making them wait as long as possible for it to occur.
- Surprise: This device jolts the audience by having something unexpected happen—either out of the blue, or after first suggesting that one thing will happen and then, when the time comes, doing something completely different. Surprise can be used to create jumps, screams, or laughs.
- Flashbacks: An expository tool in which the narrative jumps briefly back to an earlier point in the story (or to a

point before the story begins) to introduce an important plot point or piece of information.

- Cutaways (a.k.a. Asides): This device serves the same purpose a flashback, but instead of going back in time, the story jumps briefly to another location in the world of the story.

- Nonlinear Storytelling: Presenting the events of a story in nonsequential, nonchronological order. Note: It is vital that the events of a nonlinear story make sense when the narrative is untangled. Therefore, if you want to tell a nonlinear tale, it is recommended that you write it out in chronological fashion first and then chop it up.

- Narration: A disembodied voice heard on the soundtrack that advances the story by filling in gaps in the plot; explaining the characters' motives or the meaning of a scene; or commenting on the action. The narrator can be a character from the story or an omniscient/omnipresent third party.

- Voice-Over: The disembodied voice of a character heard on the soundtrack over the action of a scene. Voice-overs are used to convey the dialogue of a character who is in a scene but not on camera, or as a way of externalizing a character's inner thoughts.

- Montages: A series of brief events or images assembled into a single sequence to make a dramatic point—often to show the development of a specific skill or situation over time, or to show the variety of different ways a specific story point is being implemented.

- Intercutting: A sequence that moves back and forth between two or more narrative strands or events to make a dramatic point. Often used to create suspense or tension.
- Cards/Crawls: Two methods of using printed text to provide exposition. A card is single block of text that appears on a blank screen or over an establishing shot. A crawl is a lengthy block of moving text that rolls up over a blank screen or an establishing shot.
- Superimposed Titles: A single line of text that appears on screen over the action, usually to identify a date or location.

Devices should always be used in a way that is narratively or thematically relevant. The nonlinear/reverse-chronological plotting in Christopher Nolan's *Memento* perfectly mirrored the protagonist's efforts to retrace his steps so he could regain his lost memories—an ideal marriage of form and function. In contrast, the flashbacks to the murder of Dr. Kimble's wife in *The Fugitive* were used arbitrarily to jazz up the storytelling. Nothing in the story's theme or narrative required such an approach and, while it was effective in the short run, it ultimately diluted the tale's urgency by taking far too long to explain why Kimble was searching for the one-armed man.

Avoid using devices just to use them or because they are trendy or cool. A device used purposefully is a legitimate storytelling technique; a device used for its own sake or as a cover for weak writing (as is often the case with narration and flashbacks) is simply a gimmick. Technique enhances a story; gimmicks distract from it (and so can quickly become tiresome).

If a device is used, it should be used consistently throughout the story, rather than just on occasion to patch over rough spots.

SUPPORTING CHARACTERS

You will need characters other than the Protagonist and the Antagonist to tell your story. These supporting characters must serve a specific purpose in the narrative—they must play a specific role. The most common roles supporting characters play are:

- The Mentor: This character helps the Protagonist come into his own by introducing him to new ideas and philosophies; by teaching him new skills; by helping him develop his innate talents; by guiding him through new and unfamiliar situations; and by encouraging him to fulfill his destiny. Merlin, Yoda, and Obi-Wan Kenobi are classic Mentor characters.

- The Ally: Someone who assists the Protagonist in his quest to achieve his goal. The Ally often has a special skill or knowledge that comes in handy during the quest. Matt Hooper in *Jaws*, Sallah in *Raiders of the Lost Ark* and Ali Kerim Bey in *From Russia with Love* are all memorable allies.

- The Cause: A character who provides the Protagonist with a reason for pursuing his goal—a sick child for whom a cure needs to be found; a kidnapped love interest who needs to be rescued; a missing dog that needs to be found, etc. *Die Hard*'s Holly McClane is an ideal Cause.

- The Sounding Board: Someone—a best friend, a lover, an assistant, a sidekick, etc.—the Protagonist can talk to in order to voice his thoughts and feelings. Jeff, the roommate character played by Bill Murray in *Tootsie*, and Al Powell in *Die Hard* are effective Sounding Boards.

- The Example: Someone the Protagonist interacts with to show a different side to his personality—to demonstrate that the Protagonist can be warm or tough or fun, serious, resilient, etc. This is often the role a love interest or a child plays in a story. The refugee couple Rick helps in *Casablanca* are an excellent Example.

- The Henchman: An assistant to the Antagonist—someone who can serve as a sounding board for the main baddie and do his dirty work. Oddjob in *Goldfinger*, Mr. Joshua in *Lethal Weapon*, and Darth Vader in *Star Wars* are all classic Henchmen.

- The Explainer: A resource who provides the Protagonist with information, insight, or understanding—a boss, a teacher, an expert, an adviser, a witness, etc. The imam in *Raiders*, the Oracle in the *Matrix* series, and Deep Throat in *All the President's Men* are solid Explainers.
- The Supplier: A character who gives the Protagonist a special talisman, implement, or piece of equipment that will help him carry out his quest. James Bond's Q is the quintessential supplier.

CHARACTER DEVELOPMENT

It's one of the oldest sayings in dramatic writing, and also one of the truest: action is character—a movie character is defined solely by the things he or she says and does on-screen. The actions a character takes in a movie should reflect his goals and aspirations. The style of his actions should reflect his personality (a rough character should argue, fight, and drive recklessly; a meek character should agree, compromise, and operate with care and precision). A character's actions should display his emotions (a happy character laughs, a sad character cries, and so on).

Develop every character to the fullest. In addition to their arcs and story functions, give them each unique personalities—specific traits, eccentricities, and attitudes that complement their roles in the story and make them as distinct and memorable as possible. Their behavior should also be specific—*how* characters do things is just as telling as what they do.

Characters should always behave in ways consistent with who they are. Their personalities should not change just because it is convenient for the plot—e.g., a stupid character should not suddenly become clever just because the plot needs him to figure something out. The plot and scenes should be changed to accommodate the character, not the other way around.

All characters require strong motivation—there should be a clear and logical reason for everything a character says and does, even if it is not revealed at the time of the action.

How a character is introduced is vitally important. The things a character says and does the first time we see him will cement how we think about him for the rest of the film. So if you want your character to be tough, introduce him doing something tough; if you want him to be tender, introduce him doing something tender. Do not make the mistake many novice screenwriters do and introduce a character behaving in an atypical manner: "Carrie is usually calm, cool, and collected, but today she is stressed out and overwhelmed." Viewers judge every subsequent piece of character development against that initial introduction. If you introduce your cop protagonist in a bone-crunching fight with a group of bad guys and later show him adopting a stray puppy, we're going to think of him as a badass who is capable of being a softy. However, if you show him adopting the puppy first and getting into the bone-crunching fight later, we're going to think of him as a softy who can man up when the situation warrants. These are two very different characterizations developed out of the same basic material. Make sure you present your character correctly from the get-go.

While you certainly should make all your characters as interesting and colorful as you can, do not allow the supporting characters to become more interesting or more colorful than the Protagonist, who should always be at the center of our attention. Supporting characters don't have the burden of carrying the plot, so you are free to riff with them in ways you cannot with the Protagonist, and it can sometimes be easy to get carried away with them. This is often a problem with the villains in action and fantasy movies, who tend to be larger than life anyway. It's okay to let them go a little over the top, but don't let them go so far over that they end up stealing the movie (as happened in the first four Batman movies).

Many scripts, especially genre stories, employ stock characters: stereotyped figures that have appeared hundreds of times in similar stories and so are instantly recognizable to viewers without extensive explanation or development.

Common stock movie characters include: the rebel cop who works alone and doesn't play by the rules; the super-capable career woman who is a disaster in her personal life; the evil mastermind bent on world domination; the crude, obnoxious wingman of the male lead in a romantic comedy; the hostile, man-hating best friend of the female lead in a romantic comedy; the gruff police captain who yells all the time; the horny or rapping or slang-talking grandma. Stock characters are used so often because they are dependable and effective and don't require too much heavy lifting on the part of the screenwriter to make an impact. However, because they've been used so much, they've become tired and clichéd. So avoid using stock characters if at all possible. If you do use them, give them some sort of fresh spin to take the edge off of their familiarity.

DIALOGUE

Each character should speak in a unique voice—with unique cadence, rhythm, diction, attitude, and sense of humor. No two characters should speak or sound alike, since no two people in real life do. The way a character talks should reflect his or her personality.

Dialogue can be naturalistic or it can be stylized. If you want your characters to speak naturally, then the dialogue should reflect the way people speak in real life—speeches should be short (most real people don't speak in five-page monologues, so your characters shouldn't either), informal (unless a scene warrants formality), and indirect (people usually don't say exactly what they mean—they tend to talk around a point, meander, digress. Your characters should do the same). If you opt to take a stylized approach, that's fine—as long as the stylization is consistent throughout the script and is not so far out as to be incomprehensible.

THE WORLD OF THE STORY

Every screen story takes place in its own unique world. That world can be a specific time and place (prehistoric Africa, medieval France, present-day New York City); it can be a particular society, profession, or field of endeavor (the world of Park Avenue debutantes, the world of high finance, the world of ice yachting); it can be an imaginary fantasy land (postapocalyptic New Jersey, Oz, Krypton, Hell).

Whatever that world is, it must be established in Act I. All relevant aspects and elements of the world—its environment, its technology, its manners and customs and protocols—must be clearly explained to the audience through appropriate imagery and dramatic action. The more exotic and unusual the arena is, the more explanation is required (we all know how a toaster works, but most of us probably don't understand the intricacies of high finance or experimental brain surgery). This is especially true if the story takes place in a wholly invented fantasy world (we're not going to know what a Fourth-Level Blondarf on the planet Lemilac is unless you tell us). When it comes to unusual or imaginary worlds, never assume viewers will understand anything unless you clearly spell it out—they will not. Do not be afraid of overexplaining things—excessive detail can always be trimmed, but the confusion that comes from too little information can't be made up for.

THE REALITY OF THE STORY

Every screen story takes place in its own unique reality. *The Hurt Locker* takes place in a reality that approximates our own—in which bombs and bullets have deadly consequences and the laws of physics apply. In contrast, the *Lethal Weapon* movies take place in a reality in which people can be shot at by thousands of rounds of ammunition and never get hit; in which they can jump off tall buildings and never get hurt; and in which they can outrun massive explosive fireballs and never get singed. Movies can conjure up myriad realities: in *Death Wish*, there are muggers and rapists waiting around every corner; in *Crouching Tiger, Hidden Dragon*, people can run up walls and leap across treetops; in *The Avengers*, superheroes are commonplace; in *Star Wars*, spaceships can maneuver like fighter planes; and in *The Godfather*, criminals operate by a strict code of honor.

A story's reality must be established at the beginning of the script—i.e., if your story takes place in a reality in which cars fly, then we must learn that those cars can fly on page 1, not on page 57. Once established, that reality must be maintained consistently from the beginning of the story to the end—i.e., if a single bullet can kill a person in Act I, then your hero cannot get shot twenty-seven times and live in Act III. Viewers will generally go along with any parameters that you establish, but if you violate them, they will feel cheated and you will lose them. Everything that happens in a story must be believable within that story's reality.

EXPOSITION

Exposition is the background information—character histories, important events that occurred prior to the beginning of the story, technical information—the audience needs to know to understand the story.

All exposition must be dramatized. Many beginning screenwriters make the mistake of writing exposition into their screenplays in the same way an author would write it into a novel:

> A man walks into the bank. This is Fred Johnson, an ex-cop turned private investigator who is on the run after being framed for murder by his partner. The only way Fred can clear his name is to find the one witness who saw his partner

commit the murder. The witness's name is Maggie Morrisette, and she is currently hiding out in Paris. Fred has come
into the bank to secure a loan that will allow him to fly to
France and search for the elusive Morrisette.

As vital as this information is, none of it will be communicated to viewers, because they can't read the screenplay.
They can only see what is happening on-screen, and in this
case, all they will see is a man walk into a bank. To communicate exposition to the audience, it must be presented
in a combination of action, images, and dialogue. In the
example above, the information regarding Fred's backstory
could be turned into scenes: we could see the partner kill
the victim and frame Fred; we could see Fred run from the
cops; we could see him discover the identity of the witness;
etc. These scenes could be presented at the beginning of the
story as a prologue or introduced later in the tale through
flashbacks. Other possible approaches: Fred could tell his
story to an ally or tell it to us in a voice-over or narration.
The exposition could also be presented on a card or crawl
at the beginning of the script.

All important exposition must be introduced as early in
the script as possible—in Act I or the first part of Act II—so
that the audience will be able to understand and follow the
narrative clearly from the get-go. Except for information
that cannot be revealed until the end so as not to ruin the

story (e.g., the revelation of the killer's identity and motive at the climax of a whodunit, or the villain's explanation of his master plan in the final scenes of a thriller or an action movie), no significant exposition should ever be introduced in Act III. By then, a screen story should be racing toward its climax and taking the audience along with it. If you stop at that point to explain something, you will ruin the momentum and yank viewers out of the tale at the very moment they should be most engrossed in it.

Exposition should be kept to a minimum—the audience should be given only the information it needs to clearly comprehend the story. Nonvital or irrelevant background should not be included in the script. For example, in the story cited above, we need to know that Fred is a PI, but we do not need to know he enjoys baking cherry pies to give to all his friends at Christmas.

Try not to deliver exposition in heavy-handed fashion: avoid "info dumps"—scenes in which one character shares the required background with another in a lengthy, run-on speech. Also avoid long cards, endless crawls, and an overabundance of explanatory flashbacks. Instead, deliver exposition in subtle and indirect ways. An excellent example of indirect exposition is the communication of Rick's backstory in *Casablanca*. Rather than have a scene in which Rick spells out what his life was like before he came to North Africa, the screenwriters made an amusing game out of it by having Captain Renault continually ask Rick speculative questions about his mysterious past, questions Rick refuses to answer. Through Renault's questions, we learn everything we need to know about Rick's history and are thoroughly entertained besides.

If you find that you cannot get your story started without incorporating reams and reams of exposition about the events that took place prior to the beginning of the narrative into the early sections of the script, then it is likely that you have started your story too late. If this happens, consider beginning your story at an earlier point in time.

CHAPTER 7

Some Essential Principles of Screen Storytelling

Cinema is a visual/audio medium. When we watch a movie, we can only know what we see and what we hear. Therefore, every element in a screen story must be dramatized and presented in a combination of action, images, and dialogue. Many beginning screenwriters put a lot of effort into describing what their characters are thinking and feeling. All that effort is wasted. Unlike a novel, there can be no interior storytelling in a screenplay—what a character thinks and feels will not show up on-screen, unless a way can be found to externalize those thoughts and feelings through action (crying, laughing, punching a wall) or dialogue (by having the character speak his thoughts and feelings aloud to himself, to others, or to us in narration or a voice-over).

Cinematic storytelling must be active—we should see the major events in the story happen, rather than hear about them happening. The only thing more boring and less cinematic than watching two characters talk about an exciting event we haven't seen is to hear that unseen event described in narration or voice-over. Should you consider presenting events in this fashion, always keep in mind one of the cardinal rules of screenwriting: Whenever possible—show, don't tell.

Cinematic characters must be active—they should do things rather than talk about doing things.

The cause and effect in a movie plot should always be strong—every event in a dramatic narrative should come about as a direct and logical result of the events that have preceded it. Plot development should never rely on convenience or coincidence.

When writing a fantasy, be sure to include sufficient reality. Because its core element is the photography of real people, places, and things, cinema is essentially a realistic medium, and viewers will always approach a movie using the real world as a frame of reference. Any move away from reality will require the audience to suspend its disbelief. Viewers will usually accept one step away from the real world (e.g., a man becomes a werewolf) with relative ease, because there is still sufficient reality for them to connect with as they attempt to make their way into the story. They may have difficulty accepting more than one step away (a man becomes a werewolf . . . and then travels to Mars to battle aliens) because each additional step requires them to work harder and harder to suspend their disbelief and gives them less and less reality to hold on to. If the effort becomes too much, viewers will become lost and confused and will ultimately give up on the whole thing.

Movie stories must be focused. A screenplay should never have more than one premise. (Many beginning screenwriters try to incorporate multiple premises into their scripts—"a homeless man wins the lottery . . . and then is falsely accused of murder . . . and then reunites with the daughter he abandoned years ago"—which always results in an unintelligible mishmash of multiple protagonists, antagonists, catalysts, catastrophes, and climaxes.) Also, screenplays should not have an excess of characters or subplots, and what subplots there are should not be so elaborate or complex that they overwhelm the main story.

A screen story needs to be told from a specific point of view—either through the eyes of a single character or from a third-person perspective—and that point of view must remain consistent throughout the story. For example, if you are writing a detective story told from the detective's point of view, this means the audience can only learn what the detective learns at the time he learns it. It also means you cannot cut away to show us some piece of information the detective is not privy to, even if doing so would make it a lot easier to tell the story.

Do not let the audience get ahead of your characters. If the viewers know things the people on-screen do not, they will grow bored waiting for the characters to catch up.

The tone of a screen story needs to be specific and consistent. You can choose any tone you like—your script can be deadly serious, or light and humorous, or dark and grim, or broad and silly, or gritty and realistic, or outrageous and campy. However, once you have selected a tone, you must stick with it—you cannot write a dark and grim thriller with a campy protagonist; you cannot begin as a drama and end as a farce; you cannot intercut realism and fantasy. Such inconsistencies are extremely jarring and will pull the audience right out of the story.

Every element in a screen story must have a purpose—every character, plot point, scene, bit of exposition, and storytelling device must support the script's narrative, theme, or both. Any element that does not should be removed—there should be no extraneous, irrelevant, or purposeless characters, story elements, or devices in a screenplay.

A screen story must be unified—every element in the piece must relate in some fashion to the narrative or the theme. Any element that does not should be removed. Pacing is enormously important in a screenplay—every scene and sequence should be as crisp and tight as you can possibly make it.

A screenplay must be practical—it must be able to be produced on a reasonable budget and schedule for its genre.

Make the most of every element in your screenplay—every character and narrative possibility should be developed as fully as possible, mined as much as possible, and exploited as much as possible. Every element introduced in Act I must pay off by Act III.

Make sure your script delivers what it promises: if it's a comedy, make sure it's as funny as you can possibly make it; if it's a drama, make it as moving as you can; if it's a horror film, be sure it is really scary; and so on.

Communicate clearly: the ultimate task of a movie is to engage viewers so you can make your dramatic point to them. To do this successfully, your story and script must be accessible. This does not mean you have to pander or dumb down your material, only that you let the audience in. Movies can certainly be complex, but they are not always good at being complicated—if you make your script too involved in construction or narrative, viewers may not be able to find an entry point into the story. Likewise, ambiguity and open-endedness are fine, but if you are too obscure and esoteric, audiences will be kept at arm's length and your point will never get across.

Believe in what you write. If you do, the audience will as well.

CHAPTER 8

Screenplay Format, Style, and Length

FORMAT

Screenplays are written in 12-point Courier font with a 1.5-inch margin on the left and a 1-inch margin on the right.

All screenplays begin with:

```
FADE IN:
```

This is followed by the first Scene Heading, or Scene Slug. The heading tells us if the scene takes place inside—INT. (for "interior")—or outside—EXT (for "exterior"); the name of the location; and whether the scene occurs during the day or at night. The heading is always written in CAPS:

```
INT. GRAND CENTRAL STATION—NIGHT
```
or
```
EXT. PASADENA CITY HALL—DAY
```

A new slug is used every time there is a change in location (even if it is only from one room in a building to another room in the same building) or time.

When characters move directly from one location to an adjoining location, with no break in time or action, the DAY/NIGHT segment of the second heading is replaced by the term CONTINUOUS:

```
INT. BEDROOM—NIGHT

Gina is dozing in bed. Suddenly, the baby
begins crying (O.S.). Concerned, Gina gets
out of bed and hurries into the

INT. NURSERY—CONTINUOUS

where she lifts the baby out of his cradle
and hugs him.
```

The heading can be extended to make it more specific (e.g. to indicate a small location within a bigger one):

```
INT. PLAZA HOTEL—LOBBY—NIGHT
```

However, the slug should not be used as a descriptive or narrative device:

```
INT. BILLY'S CAR—DRIVING DOWN I-95 FROM
BOSTON TO NEW YORK—ON HIS WAY TO A NEW LIFE
AFTER BREAKING UP WITH SALLY AND LANDING
HIS DREAM JOB—EARLY MORNING—JUST PRIOR TO
THE FIRST LIGHT OF DAWN
```

The heading is followed by the Action Line (a.k.a. Stage Directions). This is the text of the scene—a written description of the dramatic action that occurs in the specified location. The Action Line indicates what characters are present when the scene begins, what characters enter, and which ones exit. It details what the characters do in the scene, the props they use, and any other relevant action or effects:

```
Sam Spade enters the office. He crosses to
the safe, dials the combination, pulls open
the door, and removes a bundle wrapped in
a velvet cloth. Spade unwraps the bundle,
revealing the MALTESE FALCON.
```

When a character speaks, his or her name is written in caps and placed at the 3.5-inch mark. Parentheticals—directions indicating how the speech is to be performed—are placed on the following line at the 3-inch mark. The dialogue itself is written below in a 3-inch-wide column starting at the 2.5-inch mark.

```
                HAMLET
                (pensive)
     To be, or not to be: that is the
     question. Whether 'tis nobler in
     the mind to suffer the slings and
     arrows of outrageous fortune. Or to
     take arms against a sea of troubles
     and by opposing end them.
```

If the dialogue is narration or a voice-over, place a (V.O.) next to the character's name:

```
                    SYDNEY (V.O.)
        It was the best of times, it was
        the worst of times.
```

If the character who speaks is part of the scene, but does not appear on camera (e.g., if she is in another room), place an (O.S.)—for "off-screen"—next to the character's name.

```
                    MOM (O.S.)
        Andrew? Is that you?
```

If you want to superimpose a title on the scene, use a partial slug as follows:

```
SUPER TITLE: Athens, 1862
```

Cards are written in similar fashion:

```
CARD: On February 12, 1809, a boy was born
in a one-room log cabin in Hardin County,
Kentucky. As an adult, that boy would save
his country and free a race of people from
enslavement. His name was Abraham Lincoln.
```

Crawls are formatted in the same style as dialogue:

```
                    CRAWL
        In the summer of 1906, a young man
        left the small Irish town of his
        birth and began a long journey to
        America in search of freedom and
        fortune.
```

On occasion, a close-up of a specific prop or action is required to make a story point. This is called an "insert" and is scripted as follows:

```
INT. LABORATORY—NIGHT

Dr. Finkelstein pours a beaker of blue
liquid into a test tube full of red liquid.

INSERT—TEST TUBE

As the blue liquid mixes with the red, a
chain reaction begins. The mixture bubbles
up and over the lip of the tube.

BACK TO SCENE

Finkelstein leaps back as the mixture
spills onto the table and begins to burn
through it.
```

When a scene is finished, we transition to the next scene. Traditionally, the transition

```
CUT TO:
```

has been used to indicate an immediate chronological move
from one scene to another. In recent years, however, that
term has been used less frequently because the transition
is assumed (a movie is going to cut from one scene to the
next whether the script tells it to or not) and not including
it saves valuable page space. To indicate that some time has
gone by between the end of the first scene and the beginning of the second, the transition

```
DISSOLVE TO:
```

is used. To indicate that a considerable period of time has
elapsed between Scene 1 and Scene 2, use

```
FADE OUT:
                                                     FADE IN:
```

Montage sequences are initiated with a partial heading,
followed by the component scenes:

```
MONTAGE:
INT. GYM—DAY
Rocky does one-armed push-ups.
```

```
INT. MEAT LOCKER—NIGHT

Rocky pummels a large carcass.

INT. MUSEUM—DAY

Rocky runs up the museum steps.

END MONTAGE
```

Intercut sequences are laid out in similar fashion:

```
INTERCUT:

EXT. EASTBOUND TRAIN TRACKS—NIGHT

The Minnesota Flyer rockets down the
tracks, heading east.

EXT. WEST BOUND TRAIN TRACKS—NIGHT

The Chicago Express rockets down the
tracks, heading west.

EXT. EAST BOUND TRAIN TRACKS—NIGHT

The Minnesota Flyer approaches a bridge.

EXT. WEST BOUND TRAIN TRACKS—NIGHT

The Chicago Express approaches the same
bridge from the opposite direction. A
collision is imminent.

END INTERCUT
```

After the final scene of the story is concluded, the script ends with one last

                                        FADE OUT:

To see how it all lays out, here is a brief excerpt from a properly formatted screenplay:

FADE IN:

EXT. NEW YORK CITY—DAY

An establishing shot of Manhattan.

                    ADULT BENJY (V.O.)
          When I was young, I believed the
          world to be a place of limitless
          possibilities.

EXT. FIFTH AVENUE—DAY

Eight-year-old BENJY MORAN walks up the
street, accompanied by his MOM and DAD.
They come to a corner and, as they wait for
the light to change, Benjy looks up and
sees

THE EMPIRE STATE BUILDING, rising 102
stories into the Manhattan sky.

An excited Benjy has to lean very far back
to take it all in.

                    BENJY
          Is that it, Dad?

                         DAD
          It sure is, buddy.

                         BENJY
                    (awestruck)
          Wow!

The light changes and the Morans cross the
street, walking towards the ESB.

SUPER TITLE: New York, 1979

MONTAGE:

INT. EMPIRE STATE BUILDING—LOBBY—DAY

The Morans enter the gorgeous art deco
lobby.

INT. EMPIRE STATE BUILDING—VISITOR'S
CENTER—DAY

Benjy and Mom wait as Dad buys some tickets
from a TELLER at a window sporting a sign
that says: "Observatory Tickets."

INT. ELEVATOR

Benjy and his folks ride in the elevator
along with a group of other TOURISTS.
Indicator lights count off the floors: 66,
67, 68 . . .

END MONTAGE

INT. EMPIRE STATE BUILDING—86TH FLOOR
OBSERVATORY—DAY

The Morans emerge from the elevator.
Excited, Benjy runs to the panoramic

```
windows and looks out in wonder at the
breathtaking aerial view of the city.
```

```
                                   DISSOLVE TO:
```

There are numerous screenwriting programs available that can assist you with properly formatting your screenplay. Final Draft is the program most commonly used in the film industry. Others include Movie Magic Screenwriter and Practical Scriptwriter.

STYLE

Action lines should be written in a clean and simple style—avoid fancy, flowery wording. A screenplay is not litera-ture—it does not derive its effectiveness from the way the author uses language. It is a descriptive document, and so its words should be used to provide as clear and direct a presentation of the action as possible. Therefore:

```
A light rain is falling.
```

is preferable to:

```
Sparkling drops of oxygenated hydrogen
tumble down from the gloomy, oppressive sky
like the bitter tears of a disappointed
lover.
```

Action should be written in short paragraphs—to make it easy to read and to simulate the energy you want the scene to have on-screen. (A series of brief items can be read at a quick, lively pace, which is presumably how the scene should play in the finished movie.) Avoid long blocks of solid type—producers, directors, actors, development executives, and readers hate them because they are a chore to slog through. Always leave plenty of white space on the page.

Do not attempt to direct the movie on paper. It is your job to tell the story—it is the job of the director (in collaboration with his or her creative team) to interpret it. Therefore:

- Except for establishing shots (which are a storytelling tool rather than a directorial one), do not write specific shots (close-ups, long shots, etc.), camera angles, or camera moves into the script—the director will determine these things in conjunction with the cinematographer.
- Avoid excessive use of inserts.
- Do not describe your characters in elaborate detail ("Lance is five feet, three inches tall, with red hair, green eyes, freckles, and a mole on his left cheek"). It's a waste of time—the director will cast the actor he or she feels is most suitable for the role, whether that actor matches your description or not. It is better just to provide a

general but evocative impression of a character ("James Bond is cool and intimidating," "Blanche is a fading Southern belle") and leave it at that.

- Likewise, do not describe sets in intricate detail—you do not need to indicate the colors of rugs and patterns on the wallpaper and the precise numbers of chairs and tables and curtains and wineglasses. Give a general impression of the place ("a run-down waterfront bar") and let the production designer take it from there.
- Avoid excessive use of parentheticals—actors don't like to be told how to say their lines and directors will ignore them.
- Do not call for ad-libbing—that's for the director to do if he or she wants to.
- Do not indicate where titles and credits should appear.
- Do not indicate what music should be used in the film or where it should be placed.

Write the script in "master scene" format—a heading followed by a simple a description of the action, and the dialogue. Let everybody else worry about everything else.

Detail every action in the script. Many novice screenwriters summarize the action: "Joe makes dinner." These summaries are too general—they can't be acted or photographed. Instead, make the action as specific as possible: "Joe puts the chicken in the oven and then returns to the counter and begins to dice the carrots," and so on.

Do not write exposition into the action lines. As stated previously, the audience can't read the screenplay, so all information must be dramatized through action, images, and dialogue.

The first time a character appears in a script, his or her name is written in CAPS. Important props, significant sound and visual effects, and important bits of action are also written in CAPS. So are descriptions of shots and camera moves, if you choose to use them (which, for the reasons explained above, you shouldn't).

When writing dialogue:

- Don't summarize conversations—e.g., "They discuss philosophy." Instead, write out every word you want the characters to say.
- Don't write out accents or dialect phonetically—no matter how well intentioned, this always reads as comical or racist. Simply write down what you want the characters to say and let the actors do the rest.
- Do not number scenes. Numbers are only used in production drafts and are inserted by the production management team.

LENGTH

On average, one page of script takes one minute to play on screen; therefore, the script for a feature film should run somewhere between 90 and 120 pages, with 110 pages being the current industry ideal. Adaptations might run a bit longer, depending on source material, but original specs should never run more than 120 pages.

CHAPTER 9

The Screenwriting Process

There are nine basic steps to crafting a screenplay:

1. Assemble Your Tools

The first step in writing anything is to gather your implements. Most screenwriters today work on a computer (often employing special screenwriting programs such as Final Draft). However, a good number still prefer to use a pen and paper, and a few even continue to use typewriters.

2. Outline

The outline is the written skeleton of your story—the document in which you lay out the plot. Many screenwriters create very detailed, formal outlines, complete with numbered and lettered headings and subheadings. Some simply make a list of the basic story points (a.k.a. "beats") called a step sheet or a beat sheet. Others jot down each beat on an individual index card and then shuffle the cards around until they find a satisfactory shape for their tale.

3. Treatment

A treatment is a screen story written in prose form, with little or no dialogue. A treatment is more developed than an outline and allows you to flesh out the narrative and characters in greater detail, as well as set a specific tone for the piece. Some treatments are just a few pages long; others are almost as long as a finished screenplay.

4. Rough Draft

The Rough Draft is the first full iteration of your story in screenplay form. No matter how finely honed your outline and treatment are, the rough draft is usually a messy document—the narrative and storytelling are often awkward; key components can be underdeveloped, illogical, or unclear; and there are frequently too many ideas, too many characters, and too much plot (for this reason, the Rough Draft is often referred to as the Kitchen Sink Draft, the S**t Against the Wall Draft, or the Vomit Draft). That's okay—the purpose of writing the Rough Draft is not to produce a finished piece of work; it is simply to get your ideas down on paper—to generate the raw material from which the final script will be created.

5. First Rewrite

"Writing is rewriting," the saying goes, and it's true—rewriting is how you transform the raw material of the Rough

Draft into a viable screenplay. It is the process by which the story and theme are focused; rudimentary characters and dialogue are transformed into flesh-and-blood people and speech; and extraneous elements are pared away. Some writers do a single extensive revision to their initial draft; others do numerous passes. There's no correct way other than to do whatever you have to do to get it right.

Once you have produced a solid "first" draft of your screenplay, it is time to get some feedback on your work.

6. Feedback

Obtaining feedback is a key part of the writing process. Your screenplay's primary task is to communicate your creative concepts and ideas to others—first to potential buyers and backers; then to the creative team tasked with bringing the piece to the screen; and finally to an audience—so it is vital to assess how good a job the script is doing of getting your points across.

- The most direct way to get feedback is to give your script to a few fellow writers or others whose taste and judgment you respect and whom you can trust to give you an honest opinion. (Giving it to multiple readers is crucial, because one person's opinion is just that, but if several people have the same reaction to the same points, then you have a much better idea of where you stand.) Once your readers have completed their task, ask them questions: What parts of the script did they like? What parts did they have problems with? Why didn't those parts work for them? Was any anything in the piece confusing or unclear? Did they care about the characters? Was there any element they wanted more of? Less of? Was the ending satisfying? When analyzing the responses, look for points of consensus—if most of your readers agree that a specific part of the script works well, you're probably in good shape. If most have a problem with a specific part, you've probably got more work to do.

• Another way to determine how well your screenplay is working is to hold a reading. Gather an enthusiastic group of participants around a table, assign each a part, and then have them read the script aloud with as much energy as they can muster while you sit back and take it all in. Having your script brought to life in such a vibrant and three-dimensional way will help you accurately assess if the story is flowing properly; if the characters and relationships are real and believable; and if the dialogue sounds natural or stilted. If possible, record the reading so you can reference it later on.

• Expert feedback can also be obtained by submitting your script to a professional script consultant—an experienced screenwriter, development executive, or teacher who will assess your work and provide you with comprehensive notes for revising it. Or you can use a script evaluation service—a company that employs professional film industry readers and development people to analyze your work from both a creative and commercial perspective. (If you are considering using a consultant or an evaluation service, check their credentials to make sure the analysts have professional industry experience. Most consultants and evaluation services are legitimate, but there are some fly-by-night folks out there, and it's always better to be safe than sorry.)

Whatever avenue you choose, the most important thing to do when you receive feedback is to listen to it, especially if it is negative. While it is certainly difficult to hear that something you've worked so hard on is not one hundred percent perfect, it's imperative that you not become defensive or resistant, because such attitudes will get in the way of the ultimate goal—to produce the best script possible.

7. Second Rewrite

Use the feedback you've received as a guide to help you revise your material—to enhance what works and to fix any problems. As you rewrite, be ruthless—don't just tweak the script here and there, but be brave enough to tear it apart: revising where necessary, rethinking where necessary, and cutting where necessary, even if it means eliminating bits you really love. (In such instances, it's best to remember the old writing adage: "In order to succeed, you must first kill all your darlings.")

8. Do It Again

Repeat Steps 5 and 6 as many times as necessary until the script is as good as it can be.

9. Presentation Draft

Once you have completed the creative work on your screenplay, you must then prepare a version to send out into the world. Begin by proofreading the piece carefully—double- and triple-checking the spelling, grammar, and formatting—from page one to page last. It is important to do this so that the script looks professional and so there's nothing in the piece to distract readers (and potential buyers) or prevent them from focusing on the content. If you're not confident of your skills in this area, consider using a professional proofreader because, as the saying goes, "You never get a second chance to make a first impression." When you have finished proofing, create a title page with the title of the script positioned in the center of the page eighteen spaces from the top, your byline placed two spaces below, and your contact info in the lower left corner. Then print several neat, clean copies of the script and prepare a PDF file, since many companies and organizations now require submissions to be made electronically.

Many screenwriters follow these nine steps exactly; others combine them (outlining the plot as they craft the treatment, refining the rough draft as they write it, etc.), and some skip a few altogether (e.g., a lot of scribes don't bother with outlines or treatments at all, but instead just dive right into writing the screenplay and figure things out as they go). Once again, there is no one correct way to go about it—the way that works best for you is the right way.

CHAPTER 10

After the Script Is Finished . . .

If your screenplay is an assignment, then turn it in to the producer or company that gave you the commission. If it's an auteur script, begin looking for backing. If your screenplay is a spec, it's time to begin the process of submitting it to the film industry—either as a writing sample to help you land an assignment, or as a property to sell to a producer or studio.

As anyone who has ever tried knows, this is not an easy thing to do. Most production companies and studios will not accept unsolicited scripts (screenplays submitted cold by writers they don't know). They abide by this policy primarily to protect themselves from lawsuits should they produce a film based on an idea similar to one contained in an unsolicited spec. (This is not an uncommon occurrence, since there are usually dozens of scripts floating around town at any one time based on the same notion—the zeitgeist works in mysterious ways.) They also use it to cut down the deluge of screenplays they might otherwise receive, as well as to screen out substandard material. Instead, production entities will usually only accept scripts submitted by established managers and agents, which means the first thing screenwriters looking to break into the industry must do is secure representation.

This can also be a difficult task. Some agents and managers are willing to accept unsolicited material from unknown writers, but most high-profile representatives are not. To break through this barrier, aspiring screenwriters must become adept at writing attention-getting query letters (and emails) that will motivate reps to request their scripts. Up-and-comers must also work hard at developing contacts—cultivating relationships with industry insiders who might be willing to recommend them and their work. (For new writers, the ability to network is just as important as the ability to spell.)

While securing an agent or manager is crucial, there are other ways you can bring your work to the attention of the industry:

- Some producers—usually those who specialize in low-budget genre films—will accept unsolicited screenplays as long as you sign a release form that frees them from any liability should they generate a similar project.
- In recent years, some production and management companies have set up web-based submission portals that allow outside writers to post a logline (a one-sentence

summary of a script's concept). If the company reps like the logline, they may ask you to send them a screenplay (along with a signed release).

- Screenwriting contests can also provide a way into the business. The Don and Gee Nicholl Fellowships in Screenwriting, an annual screenwriting competition sponsored by the Academy of Motion Picture Arts and Sciences, is very highly regarded by the industry—producers, studio executives, agents, and managers are always eager to read each year's winning scripts and top finalists. Other screenwriting competitions offer introductions to producers, agents, and managers as part of their prize packages.

- Pitching events—conferences at which aspiring screenwriters can buy five-, ten-, or fifteen-minute slots to meet with agents, managers, and production company reps to order to pitch their ideas—can also open some significant doors.

- Some screenwriting consultants and screenplay evaluation services offer to pass scripts that earn high ratings from their analysts on to industry contacts.

- There are companies that will allow you to post your script's logline to websites they claim are read by producers and development executives. Other companies send email blasts containing your logline to management and production companies throughout the industry.

The majority of screenwriting representatives, contests, consultants, and support services are legitimate and helpful. However, there are people and companies out there who aren't always honest or can't always deliver what they promise, so investigate all potential involvements thoroughly before you agree to anything or sign anything.

COPYRIGHT AND REGISTRATION

Before you send your original screenplay out into the world, copyright it with the United States Copyright Office and register it with the script registration services of either the Writers Guild of America, West, or Writers Guild of America, East. Doing this will provide you with dated legal evidence of authorship, which will come in handy should there ever be any unauthorized use of your work. (However, do not put the WGA registration number on the cover of your script—the industry considers this to be an amateurish practice.)

SUCCESS

If your spec makes it into the right hands and is positively received, there are several ways it can pay off for you:

- You can be invited to pitch original ideas to studios and production companies, and, if one sparks, be commissioned to write it.

- You can be assigned to do a rewrite on an existing script or do an adaptation of an existing property.
- Your spec can be optioned by a producer or production company. In exchange for a fee—usually a percentage of a prenegotiated purchase price—an option gives the production entity exclusive rights to your script for a limited period of time—usually six months or one year. During that period, the producers will try to set up the project (secure financing and distribution, engage a cast and creative team, etc.). If they do, then they pay you the full purchase price. If they don't, then they can renew the option (for an additional fee) or return the script to you unencumbered.
- Your spec can be purchased outright.

THE WGA

If you sell a script to or are given an assignment to write a screenplay for one of its signatory companies, you will be eligible to join the Writers Guild of America, West. The WGAW is a labor union that negotiates and enforces an employment contract with the majority of motion picture producers in the American entertainment business. This contract, called the Minimum Basic Agreement, establishes minimum fees and rates of compensation for all screen-related jobs and services. (Members are free to negotiate higher rates for their services if they can, but can not receive less than these minimums.) The WGAW also determines the writing credits on movies produced by its signatories, collects and distributes residuals, administers a health plan and a pension plan, negotiates and enforces creative and other rights, and sponsors education, outreach, and advocacy programs.

The WGAW represents screenwriters who live in both the eastern and western United States, as well as television, radio, and new-media writers who live west of the Mississippi. The Writers Guild of America, East, an affiliated but separate union, represents radio, television, and new-media writers who live east of the Mississippi. Movie scribes based in the East can also join the WGAE, but their big-screen activities remain under the jurisdiction of the WGAW. The studios and most major producers and production companies are WGA signatories and, as such, cannot employ non-WGA members on their projects (unless those writers agree to join the union once they are eligible), so if you want to work in the mainstream movie business, it behooves you to join the guild. Once you become a WGA member, you cannot work for nonsignatories.

DEVELOPMENT

Most screenplays, originals and assignments alike, go through some form of development—i.e., rewriting done to accommodate the creative wishes and ideas of the various members of the team bringing the project to life: studio executives, producers, directors, and stars. Sometimes this rewriting improves the screenplay; sometimes it does not. You might be a part of the development process or you might not be—the film business is notorious for throwing lots of writers at a single screenplay. If you're the first writer on the project, there's a good chance you'll be replaced at some point. If you're an assignment writer, you could be one of those selected to replace the original author.

The end result of development is a final draft of the screenplay (also known as a shooting script or a production draft) that contains numbered scenes and is printed on white paper. Any changes made to the script after the final draft (and, rest assured, there will be changes) will be printed on colored paper, so that the various members of the production team will be able to keep easy track of the alterations.

CREDITS

The credits on any film produced under WGA jurisdiction are officially determined by the guild. As a film nears completion, the production entity notifies the WGA and all participating screenwriters of the writing credit it plans to put on the film. If the participating screenwriters all agree with the credit, it is accepted by the union and placed on the film. If one or more of the writers objects, the matter is sent to arbitration—a team of select WGA members unrelated to the project reviews all drafts of the screenplay and determines the final credit based primarily on the percentage of material each writer is judged to have contributed to the final script. This is a crucial process not just for reasons of vanity, but also because there are often lucrative bonus and residual payments tied to receiving an on-screen credit.

GET YOUR POPCORN

If all goes well, one day you will sit down in a theater and watch your words appear on screen, translated into light, shadows, and sounds that will engage and delight audiences all over the world. That's the entire point of screenwriting—and its greatest joy!

Acknowledgements

I would like to thank Andrew Morton and Raymond J. Morton, Sr. for their technical assistance with this book.

Thanks to John Cerullo and Marybeth Keating at Hal Leonard for sparking this project and for their ongoing enthusiasm and encouragement. Thanks also to my agent, June Clark of FinePrint Literary Management, for her amazing help and support.

My deepest love to my family: Raymond J. Morton, Sr., and Rita K. Morton; Kathy, Dan, and Caitlin Hoey; Nancy and John Bevacqua; Kate, Maddie, and Carrie Lutian; Rich and Kendra Morton; William Morton; Ken Morton; Claire and Derek Masterbone; Andrew Morton; Tom, Lindsey, Erin, Jack, and Sean Morton.

Love and appreciation also to my wonderful friends: Maggie Morrisette; M.F. and Linda Harmon; Carmen and Dan Apodaca; Terri Barbagallo; Dharmesh Chauhan; James DeFelice; Gina, David, Eva, and Hugo Fénard; Brian Finn; Faith Ginsberg; Tara, Kurt, Mia, and Mattius Johnson; Richard H. Kline; Michael Larobina; Alison, John, and Bethany

Aurora Nelson; Michelle Mahana; Deborah McColl; Roger Nolan; Angel Orona; Tim Partridge; Dr. Gary Pearle; Donna and Joe Romeo; David Shaw; Steven Tropiano and Steven Ginsberg.

Finally, all my love to Ana Maria Apodaca, who is still the queen, no matter what anyone says.